WHAT PEOPLE ARE SAYING ABOUT
A WANDERER'S JOURNEY

Susan has given us a gift filled with authentic and raw truth about the realities of grief, not the brief moments of sadness but deep and lingering grief. In this missive, there is a hope that is defiant in the face of the enemy of our souls and a full surrender to the ONE who is able to sustain us in our grief and heal us all the while we are walking through pain. This book is a tool that can be used over and over again to remember, " Take heart, I have OVERCOME THE WORLD." (John 16:33b)

Portia Allen
Pastor, Co-Host for *She Speaks Stories* podcast, Co-Founder of Imago DEI Consulting

Susan is a friend and fellow sojourner into grief-laced grace. She has created an insanely practical book that will help any wanderer in grief find their way. Her vulnerability and her practicality create a space for the wounded to heal and our God who holds it all together with a good plan to shine.

Rachel Faulkner Brown
Founder and visionary of Be Still Ministries,
curator of retreats for Never Alone Widows, storyteller,
Bible teacher, Gold Star widow, wife and mom

T0005209

Susan is a kind coach, a wise friend, and a loving guide through grief, even though that's not a job most people will sign up for willingly. I'm thankful for her, her work, and for the ways I know this book is going to serve so many.

Jess Connolly
Founder of Go & Tell Gals, coach, author, speaker, podcast host

As I read the first few pages of When Grief Enters, I felt the raw familiar truth Susan Wanderer speaks about. No one likes grief, loss, or despair; yet it happens to most of us. I know grief firsthand through the loss of a child and as a licensed mental health professional. Susan gives kind, compassionate, and doable guidance to navigate the overwhelming waves. She points her readers to Jesus, but it is not trite. Knowing we are not alone in our suffering and seeing someone swimming against the current is the encouragement we all need. I look forward to sharing this resource with my clients.

Barbara Conord
Licensed Professional Counselor, Co-Founder of Kairos Counseling

Susan is a breath of fresh air, and a strong leader full of wisdom. This book will help you on the journey of grief with promises from God's Word as well as daily application. It has the ability to encourage your heart and remind you that grief isn't the end. With personal stories, she shares her heart and desire to see others overcome what hard times can create.

Tammie Floyd
Founder and Co-Senior Pastor of Lifepoint Church, Fredericksburg, VA

Every word of this is tried, tested, and true. Susan has embodied what it looks like to move through grief instead of route around it. The best example I can give: When I was engulfed in grief last year without a shred of light, Susan sent me a $10 Starbucks gift card every single Monday for six months. She didn't hustle me through my sorrow; she simply bore witness and provided the caffeine. She loved me perfectly and waited for the light to crack through. She is an absolute treasure, and this project is a gift.

Jen Hatmaker
New York Times best-selling author, host of *For the Love* podcast, speaker, and a daily friend to an incredible community of women

These are the words we've been waiting to read for years! Finally, Susan's heart has overflowed onto the page. It's like reading a text message from your best friend who knows exactly what to say. Susan's authenticity drips from every word. For every person feeling pain, walking in grief, or struggling to make it through another day, Susan will help you on the journey and point you in the right direction to take your next step.

Pastors Stu and Tab Hodges
Waters Edge Church, Hampton Roads, VA

There are authors who write based upon what they've been "taught" - book knowledge. But then, there are others who also write from the core of their heart and soul, bearing their most vulnerable experiences and emotions with the pure goal of helping readers gain the strength to pull to the next day and the day after. That is the hope and strength that you'll find in *When Grief Enters*.

Michele McKinney
Dream Champion: helping women juggle life while executing their God-given dreams and purpose

Susan Wanderer has done a remarkable job articulating the complexities, nuances, and different ways we experience grief in our lives in a way anyone can identify with. Through her book *When Grief Enters*, readers' souls will be encouraged as they become more aware of how to process grief and how grief takes on different forms. She encourages us to hold onto God's promises that He is close to the broken hearted.

Irene Rollins
Founder of TWO=ONE Marriage Ministry, recovery activist, author, public speaker

Susan Wanderer doesn't just write from a hypothetical perspective; she writes from the heart. Grief can lead us into some dark places and deeper into despair. There is a way out. There is hope. *When Grief Enters* is a real and honest look at grief, but it is also a journey of hope. If grief has gripped you or held you, it's time to take a step toward hope.

Andrew Segre
Lead Pastor at Coastal Church Chesapeake

When Grief Enters is a holistic approach to walking through the overwhelming heartbreak of grief. Susan centers processing grief around the spiritual, physical, and emotional aspects we all face and through her own beautiful story shows us how to feel our grief and also heal our grief.

Brandi Wilson
Co-Leader of Leading and Loving It, life coach, author, and speaker

A Wanderer's Journey

– Volume One –
When Grief Enters

Susan Wanderer

A Wanderer's Journey, Volume One: When Grief Enters

Copyright © 2022 by Susan Wanderer

All rights reserved. No part of this publication may be reproduced, stored in a retrieval system, or transmitted in any form or by any means – electronic, mechanical, photocopying, recording, or otherwise – except for brief quotations in printed reviews, without the prior written permission of the copyright owner.

Unless otherwise noted, all scripture references taken from

THE HOLY BIBLE, NEW INTERNATIONAL VERSION®, NIV®, Copyright © 1973, 1978, 1984, 2011 by Biblica, Inc. ™ Used by permission. All rights reserved worldwide.

Cover design by Jana White
Photography by Josh Wanderer

Print ISBN: 978-1-951022-18-1
Digital ISBN: 978-1-951022-19-8

Published by Wanderers Press
in collaboration with the Blount Collective
Printed in the United States

10 9 8 7 6 5 4 3 2 1

This little book is dedicated to my family of Wanderers
Ed, Joshua, Ruth, and Dibora.

May you always know the closeness of Jesus during all
seasons as we wander this life together.
I love you forever.

CONTENTS

THREE WAYS TO EXPERIENCE WHEN GRIEF ENTERS

1. **A Personal Devotional** – For five days, take a moment each day to sit with Jesus and this little book. Allow the words, the stories, and the scriptures to minister to your heart and your soul. Use the prayer and journal prompts at the end of each chapter to spend time with Jesus, the One who is always present during seasons of heartache.

2. **A Small Group Study** – For five weeks, gather your friends or small group and focus on one section a week. While the prayer and journal prompts will walk with you on your personal journey, you may also use these as small group questions to help facilitate your weekly discussions and prayers.

3. **Tucked Inside the Corner Nook of a Coffeeshop** – If you are in a season where the journal and prayer prompts are too much, where gathering with a small group is too hard for your grieving soul, I understand. Instead, tuck yourself away with this book and simply allow the words on the page to enter your grief and heartache. My prayer is that healing and hope will begin to find you as you turn these pages.

INTRODUCTION

Hello Friend!

I'm not an expert on grief. I don't hold a degree in counseling or psychology. It's not a subject I've spent much time researching, and I certainly never thought I would be writing about it. I'm a glass half full, walk on the positive side, enneagram seven, funny storyteller girl who doesn't often think about grief.

Then grief arrived at my front door.

Once you have lived inside the world of grief, you are never the same. Your heart beats differently, and your tears flow more often. Your love increases for your circle of people. You learn the sacredness of holding space for grief and the impact it has on you physically, spiritually, and emotionally. To ignore grief is a dangerous act. If you pretend it doesn't exist, grief will take your mind, body, and soul to places you don't want to go.

I humbly pray that this little book will serve you in some way as you walk this path of grief or are holding hands with those who are brokenhearted.

In this world, we are promised grief—but friend, take heart.

Susan

CHAPTER ONE

THE KNOWING

My undergrad degree is in human services from Carson Newman College—Dolly Parton country. I adored every single day of my time in the small town of Jefferson City, basking in the beauty of the Smoky Mountains of East Tennessee.

The people.
The mountains.
The professors.
The campus.
All of it.

My college experience was sincerely four of the best years of my life.

In my human services and sociology-focused classes, I learned about death and dying, marriage and family, deviance and social control, homelessness and poverty. ...The list was endless.

These classes made me a fascinated student of people and their cultures, and I quickly learned that one thing all of these cultures and people held in common was grief.

As a minister, I now sometimes sit at the side of men and women, teens and children as they start walking the path of grief. Other times, I hold hands with those who are fully

"

Inside the grieving,
the weeping, and
the silence, the
sacredness of the
Father's comfort
has begun.

and totally worn out from their long journey with grief as a constant companion.

I learned early on in my career that grief has different sounds. It can sometimes be an intense, deafening silence . . . a silence where no words could—or should—be uttered. During these long stretches of silence, you can feel and hear your own heart pounding. At first, there's a sense of awkwardness, and then the awkwardness dissipates and a knowing forms...a knowing that a different way of walking through life must now be discovered and learned.

Other times, the grief arrives as the cries of a mother . . . a cry that announces the absolute disgust, horror, and pain at her child leaving this earth far outside the natural order of death.

The few times I've sat with a family after the death of a child are like no other. Silence and crying intermingle inside the grief. They're heavy. They sit thick in the air and feel like a dense fog. You want to wave it away. You want to speak words, any words that will bring even an ounce of comfort. But you realize that speaking in the silence and through the cries interrupts the sacredness. Hand holding and just being present is the prayer for comfort you are offering up to God the Father.

That sacred moment is the space set aside to grieve. Inside this space is where the Father begins to minister. Most of the time, the pain is too intense to even know this is happening, but it is happening.

PRAISE BE TO THE GOD AND FATHER
OF OUR LORD JESUS CHRIST, THE
FATHER OF COMPASSION AND
THE GOD OF ALL COMFORT,
WHO **COMFORTS US IN ALL OUR
TROUBLES**, SO THAT WE CAN
COMFORT THOSE IN ANY TROUBLE
WITH THE COMFORT WE OURSELVES
RECEIVE FROM GOD.

2 Corinthians 1:3-4, NIV

"Praise be to the God and Father of our Lord Jesus Christ, the Father of compassion and the God of all comfort, who comforts us in all our troubles, so that we can comfort those in any trouble with the comfort we ourselves receive from God" (2 Corinthians 1:3-4, NIV).

Inside the grieving, the weeping, and the silence, the sacredness of the Father's comfort has begun.

For those walking in grief, may you know this sacredness. May you know His comfort.

Sojourn Stop

Father of compassion, You are the God of comfort, and You promise to comfort us in our troubles. Give us this sacred time and space to grieve on Your chest, to weep and to also sit in silence. May we know Your comfort. In the name of Jesus, amen and amen.

Reflection

1. Susan describes The Knowing in this chapter, " . . . that a different way of walking through life must now be discovered and learned." Explain your knowing moment.

2. The space set aside to grieve is sacred. The Father ministers to us while in our grief. Take a moment to write out the grieving parts of your soul.

3. Read 2 Corinthians 1:3-4 out loud, perhaps in different translations on a Bible app. Write it below slowly, soaking in each word.

4. Grief is a journey. Pray the words offered at the Sojourn Stop. Write below a more focused prayer here for your specific story.

CHAPTER TWO
THE PRESSURE

The last five years have found me sitting with people in a more intimate way — as a family member and a friend. Grief looks different here. It lasts longer. The pain is personal.

I've seen grief up close now, in myself and in the ones I love the most.

In the death of a child.
In the end of a marriage.
In the death of a spouse.
In the betrayal of a friendship.
In the loss of health.
Abuse.
Job loss.
Depression.
Addiction.

The list could go on.

So much of life can lean, twist, and turn towards grief. As we are promised in John 16:33, in this world, we will have trouble.

James Strong's *The Exhaustive Concordance of the Bible* describes the word trouble in the original text (thlip'-sis): Anguish, burdened, persecution, tribulation, trouble, pressure (literally or figuratively).

Pressure. Literally or figuratively.

These last few years, I've experienced my own grief. My own sadness. My own flowing tears. I hadn't been able to put words to what I was feeling until I read that explanation of what "trouble" meant in its original context.

The word "pressure" describes every bit of it.

Pressure in my heart.
Pressure in my relationships.
Pressure in my home.
Pressure in my marriage.
Pressure in my job.
Pressure in my body.

Sitting in grief is a daily experience of pressure. It's the pressing together of so many emotions. You feel at times that you are living inside an actual pressure cooker.

Sadness.
Loneliness.
Heartache.
Depression.
Loss.
Disappointment.

Sometimes, it's a smattering of all of them at once. Other times, it's just sadness or just heartache or just loneliness.

Nevertheless, the pressure is there. One moment the pressure is strong, and the next it's like a faint tug. But you know it's

"

At this intersection
of carrying your grief
and knowing God,
a new portion of faith
begins to form.

there. There is a knowing that this grief, however strong or faint, could be your bedfellow for a long time.

There are days when your grief seems to have passed. You are graced with a day of bright sunshine, laughter, and freedom. The heaviness is laid aside, and you feel like running through fields and singing because the hills are alive with the sound of music. Your heart feels free again. You start believing that better days could indeed be ahead.

After a hearty belly laugh, though, something shifts inside. You don't feel grief, but something equally burdensome creeps in: guilt.

Guilt links arms with grief and says, "Honey! Don't forget your luggage." Your shoulders slump. You remember to bend down, hold your back, and brace for the weight and distress of what you are about to pick up and carry again.

You close your eyes, feel the sting of hot tears, and whisper to convince yourself, "God is here. He is faithful."

The pressure and weight of grief returns, and you find yourself at an intersection. At this intersection of carrying your grief and knowing God, a new portion of faith begins to form.

This portion you wish you didn't need to experience. Yet, on the other side of this intersection, the understanding of God's love is deeper, clearer, and stronger. A greater knowledge forms as He proves how He can carry your grief and your heartache. A trust begins to form.

IN ALL THEIR DISTRESS HE TOO
WAS DISTRESSED, AND THE ANGEL
OF HIS PRESENCE SAVED THEM.
**IN HIS LOVE AND MERCY HE
REDEEMED THEM**; HE LIFTED
THEM UP AND CARRIED
THEM ALL THE DAYS OF OLD

Isaiah 63:9, NIV

"In all their distress he too was distressed, and the angel of his presence saved them. In his love and mercy he redeemed them; he lifted them up and carried them all the days of old" (Isaiah 63:9, NIV).

Friend, it may not feel like it right this very moment, but He will carry you. He will redeem these days of grief and distress.

Take a moment, relax your tired back, and allow Him to carry your luggage of grief and relieve the pressure of your troubles.

Sojourn Stop

Father of love and mercy, may we know Your presence. We are so very tired. Grief is exhausting. The pressure is overwhelming. In Your love and mercy, give us relief. Carry us as we grieve. In the name of Jesus, amen and amen.

Reflection

1. In this chapter we find the definition of trouble: Pressure, literally or figuratively. Take a few moments to write out where you are currently experiencing pressure. (Relationships, home, marriage, job, body, etc.)

2. What emotions are being pressed together because of what you listed above?

3. Read Isaiah 63:9 out loud. Write these words below slowly, focusing on every word being written.

4. Pause at the Sojourn Stop and offer up the prayer that is written. Take a moment, then relax your tired back and declare to Jesus the luggage of grief you are carrying. Allow Him to begin to relieve the pressure of your troubles.

CHAPTER THREE
THE WOUND

Americans live in a microwave culture. We expect everything to arrive, be fixed, and be ours in a quick, timely manner.

The truth is that grief does not operate in this way.

My mom, several years ago, had a wound in her back from a deep, invasive back surgery. After weeks upon weeks in the hospital and rehabilitation facility, she was ready to come home. But to come home safely, the doctors said that she needed a daily wound dresser. Declared the "Wound Dresser" and "Wound Specialist" by my family, I had to take two classes on how to dress Mom's wound each day.

I have honestly never sweated as much as I did the day my first wound class arrived. I begged God to keep my lunch in my stomach and for my hands not to shake. After those two classes, one thing was for certain: I am not meant for the medical profession.

Her wound, square in the middle of her back, was crazy deep. Each day I would take long pieces of narrow gauze and—using a utensil—begin pushing them down into her wound. I would push and feed that gauze into her back until there was no more pushing that could be done.

The next morning, I would pull the wet gauze out and apply the new. It took months to heal. I honestly never thought there would be a day my mom would not have this gaping

"

But we are
not alone in this
process, for we
have been given the
Wound Dresser.

huge hole. One day, however, I heard my Mom cheering, "It's CLOSED!"

Wounds take time to heal. The deeper they are, the longer it takes. The more complicated the grief, the lengthier the healing process.

But we are not alone in this process, for we have been given the Wound Dresser. Every day that we are in our grief and the tears begin to flow, He is there to bind our wounds.

He won't give up until our broken hearts are healed. It is the promise of Psalm 147:3: "He heals the brokenhearted and binds up their wounds" (NIV).

Sojourn Stop

Father to the brokenhearted, may we know Your healing. May we experience peace as You daily bind up our wounds. May we know You better as a result of being cared for. In the name of Jesus, amen and amen.

Reflection

1. In this chapter we talk about the depth and healing of a wound. The more complicated the grief, the lengthier the healing process. What is the wound that is causing your grief?

2. What have you noticed about your wound during your healing process? Is it taking longer to heal than you anticipated?

HE HEALS THE
BROKENHEARTED
AND **BINDS UP**
THEIR WOUNDS.

Psalm 147:3 NIV

3. Read Psalm 147:3 out loud several times. Describe what you know to be true about the Wound Dresser.

4. Spend some time at the Sojourn Stop today. After you read the prayer, take a few moments to write out a personal prayer in the space below. Ask the Wound Dresser to continue to bind your wounds.

CHAPTER FOUR

THE WORK

2020 was a tender and difficult year, one of the hardest we've known as a family.

One morning when the fog eventually lifted and brighter days were prevailing, my husband, Ed, told me he wanted to share his story. He wanted to help others know that there is hope, to know where to find it and how to experience it.

Some men would tuck the journey of mental health in their back pocket and speak of it no more. Instead, Ed wanted others to know that there is hope in seasons of deep depression.* There is help. There is never a need to suffer in silence.

During the season of depression Ed experienced, he taught me so much. Despite his sadness, I saw him do the hard work of healing. He did not sit back and be overtaken. He got to work.

He found a great therapist and a fantastic counselor. He began taking daily walks. He participated in two weeks of outpatient therapy. He found good medication. He prayed. He read scripture. He cried. He talked. He worshiped. He sat in silence.

Some days were harder than others, but he never gave up.

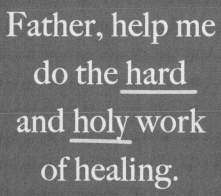

"

Father, help me
do the <u>hard</u>
and <u>holy</u> work
of healing.

He showed up in his grief with the Comforter every day and did the hard and holy work of healing.

We created a scripture wall beside his side of the bed. Most mornings—and most evenings—I would find him there, sitting on the side of the bed, reading the words and praying the prayers.

He was doing the hard work of healing.

Truth be told, when I am in the deep end of sadness, I would rather find an extra episode on Netflix and isolate myself from everyone.

There are some days that call for quiet and being alone, but this can't be the norm. Allow your people to love you, to cook for you, to be on standby phone calls, to buy you coffee and sit in silence or fill the space with talking. Don't choose to sit in loneliness and despair. They only exasperate grief.

The small community of family and friends that rose around us during Ed's season of depression were the very breath of God on our necks. They held up our arms and loved us through it. We know the love of Jesus deeper because of their unwavering kindness.

As I sit in my own sadness right now, I know this to be true: The knowing of grief may sit fresh, the pressure intense, and the wounds deep, but the work also must be done.

The tender, beautiful news about a brokenhearted person doing the hard work of healing is that they will know the

Father like never before. He does the hard work with us. He carries us, He binds our wounds, He heals our heartache.

It will take time because deep wounds take time to heal. All the while though He remains close. And His closeness is everything.

"The Lord is close to the brokenhearted and saves those who are crushed in spirit" (Psalm 34:18, NIV).

As we began this little book together with the knowledge that we will have trouble in this world, we will end it by embracing the rest of the promise: may we take heart, because He does indeed overcome (John 16:33).

Sojourn Stop

Father, help me do the hard and holy work of healing. Carry me, bind my wounds, heal my heartache, and walk the path of healing with me. In the name of Jesus, amen and amen.

*You can listen to Ed's entire story on *She Speaks Stories*, a podcast I do with some of my favorite friends each week (shespeaksstories.com, Episode #155).

Reflection

1. You are invited this week to listen in to the story of Susan's husband, Ed. He walks through his experience with depression. His episode can be found at shespeaksstories.com, Episode #155.

THE LORD IS **CLOSE**

TO THE BROKENHEARTED

AND SAVES THOSE WHO

ARE CRUSHED IN SPIRIT.

2 Corinthians 1:3-4, NIV

2. The Father does the hard work of healing with us. As you examine your wound and experience your grief, what healing-work do you need to focus on?

3. Read Psalm 34:18 out loud several times. Take a few moments to write it slowly--word for word--below in the space provided.

4. Spend time at the Sojourn Stop and pray the prayer provided. Write out your own prayer, asking God to help you do the holy and hard work of healing.

CHAPTER FIVE
THE TOOLS

After Ed's podcast episode aired, the primary question we received from people was, "What is my first step?"

Here is where we started. I pray that this list may serve you well in your own journey with grief.

1. **Counseling and Therapists:** Our counselors and therapists are an extension of our family. They speak life over us and have permission to speak the hard truth we need to hear. Ed and I are huge fans of counseling. One thing to note: If your counselor thinks you may benefit from medication, they will probably point you towards a psychiatrist. Medication is a beautiful extension of counseling and can be a helpful tool.

2. **Scripture, Prayer, and Worship:** When we are experiencing the intense pressure of grief, we sometimes find it unusually exhausting to crack open a Bible, much less find the passages that will nourish our souls and speak to our wounds. Therefore, we created a Scripture and Prayer Wall. At any moment, we can just sit, read, pray, worship, and walk away. It gives us a clear path and plan. Here is a list of some of the scriptures on our wall. They bring comfort to us and remind us that *He is for us, He is near, and He is actively helping us.*

"

I found people
that helped me
remember the
goodness of God.

Isaiah 43:1	1 Peter 1:3	2 Chronicles 20:17
Psalm 103:4-5	Isaiah 48:17	Deuteronomy 7:15
Psalm 46:1	Luke 18:1	Hebrews 4:16
Ephesians 4:20	Jeremiah 30:17	Isaiah 41:13

3. **Community:** Find your people. One thing that COVID taught me is that continued isolation can breed anxiety, grief, and depression. Community fosters hope. I have heard it said so many times, but the saying is true: we are better together. All kinds of people are good to be in your community. Good listeners. Hand holders. Do you have one in your bunch that is witty and fun? A yummy cook? Your community helps you remember that you are not alone in the journey.

I know there may be some who are desperately searching for community and need a safe landing place. You haven't found your people yet. I sincerely and deeply know this feeling.

Here is the primary place I found my people: Church. I will forever be a local church girl.

I know what you may be thinking: Church is messy, no thanks.

You are correct. Church is made up of everyday people, and it can indeed be a bit messy.

Even so, I found these beautiful moments of support, friendship, and authentic community.

While in my grief, inside my church . . .

I found deep friendships.

I found shoulders that hold my tears.

I found arms that hug tight.

I found hands that bring meals.

I found humor that provides laughter.

I found people that helped me remember the goodness of God.

My view of community is this: We have a Wound Dresser, and He is daily binding our wounds. Community are the nurses handing Him the gauze. They bring meals, send text messages, hold hands, brew coffee, show up and sit in the silence.

Community helps us overcome.

My prayer for you — God, bring near those who know Your love and will love this soul deeply and fully in return.

Sojourn Stop

Father of comfort, provide us wise counselors, speak to us through Your sacred scriptures, listen to our prayers, and form a loving community around us. In finding comfort and healing, may we in return provide comfort to those who also walk this road. In the name of Jesus, amen and amen.

Reflection

1. In this chapter we read about a list of tools. Number two is Scripture, Prayer, and Worship. Spend time diving into these scriptures that are listed. Look them up and write them out below in the space provided or on note cards.

I HAVE TOLD YOU THESE THINGS,
SO THAT IN ME YOU MAY HAVE
PEACE. IN THIS WORLD YOU WILL
HAVE TROUBLE. BUT TAKE HEART!
I HAVE OVERCOME THE WORLD.

John 16:33

Say them out loud.

Isaiah 43:1

1 Peter 1:3

2 Chronicles 20:17

Psalm 103:4-5

Isaiah 48:17

Deuteronomy 7:15

Psalm 46:1

Luke 18:1

Hebrews 4:16

Ephesians 4:20

Jeremiah 30:17

Isaiah 41:13

2. Spend some time in prayer at the Sojourn Stop. Pray the words of the prayer provided and then write a prayer below asking God to direct you as you link arms with Counselors, Scriptures, and Community.

MY PLAYLIST

During my deep season of grief, when the Bible felt too laborious to pick up, I would place the words of scripture inside my heart through music. I created a playlist that I would use while walking my neighborhood, going to sleep at night, cooking dinner, driving in my car. These songs became a battle cry and constant prayers during a very dark season.

Jesus was present during every note I offered up and every off-key verse I sang. He indeed inhabited the praises of this tired, grieving woman. My prayer is that these songs will do the same for you.

- *Jireh* by Elevation Worship and Maverick City Music
- *Wait on You* by Elevation Worship and Maverick City Music
- *Million Little Miracles* by Elevation Worship and Maverick City Music
- *Peace Be Still* by Hope Darst
- *Healing is in Your Hands* by Christy Nockles
- *Jesus, I Am Resting* by Tricia Brock

- *My Jesus* by Anne Wilson
- *Believe for It* by Cece Winans
- *I Speak Jesus* by Charity Gayle
- *Look What You've Done* by Tasha Layton
- *No One Ever Cared for Me Like Jesus* by Steffany Gretzinger
- *The God Who Sees* by Nicole C Mullen
- *More Than Anything* by Natalie Grant
- *Who Am I* by Watermark

ACKNOWLEDGEMENTS

As a first-time author, I had no understanding of the enormous task it is to bring a book to life. The writing of the words was truly just the starting point. These amazing humans have added their inspiration, wisdom, prayers, talent, and time to this project. I am sincerely so very grateful. Together they made this little book happen. I have the greatest friends and family on the planet.

Thank you to
Susan & Steve Blount
Joshua Wanderer
Jessica Chamblee
Gwen Curtis
Tess Curtis
Linda Elliot
Jana White
The *Wander On* Community
The *She Speaks Stories* Community
Ron & Beth Harvey
Dean & Kate Wanderer

Cover & Layout by Jana White

Photography by Josh Wanderer

ABOUT THE AUTHOR

Susan believes she was meant to be a confetti-popping, pom-pom-carrying, big bow-wearing, high-kicking cheerleader in her teenage years! Her biggest happy in life is to cheer others on in their gifting and watch them succeed. She met her husband (Ed) almost two decades ago on the internet, before internet dating was even a thing. Five years after they were married, they crossed an ocean to unite with their three courageous kids: Joshua, Ruth, and Dibora. These four Wanderers are the joy of her heart! Susan has been in full time ministry for almost thirty years, and is a Licensed Coach, Communicator, and Author.

Please follow Susan on...

 @SusanWanderer

 SusanHarveyWanderer

SUGGESTED RESOURCES

She Speaks Stories

God uses unique characters and complicated plot twists to weave a story with each of our lives – a story that's meant to be told and heard. We share stories that change lives on our podcast  and at our live events. To listen to the latest episode or learn about our upcoming live events, go to **shespeaksstories.com**

Wander On

No matter your goals, Wander On is a group that prioritizes community over competition. We cheer on everyone's fitness goals: whether you're trekking on a multi-day adventure or circling the block, we can't wait to see you succeed! To learn more about our community of wanderers or to join our Facebook group, go to **letswanderon.com**

WANDERERS PRESS

A Wanderer's Journey contains four volumes.

Volume One – Summer 2022
Volume Two – Fall 2022
Volume Three – Summer 2023
Volume Four – Winter 2024

To order additional copies of
this book, go to
LetsWanderOn.com/shop

eBook available at
Amazon.com

Audiobook available at
Audible.com, Amazon.com,
and iTunes